HOUSE OF CONTRASTS

Daniela Andonovska-Trajkovska

Červená Barva Press
Somerville, Massachusetts

Červená Barva Press
P.O. Box 440357
W. Somerville, MA 02144

www.cervenabarvapress.com

Bookstore: www.thelostbookshelf.com

Production: Allison O'Keefe

Cover art: Ljupka Gałązka-Vasilev

ISBN: 978-1-950063-84-0

Library of Congress Control Number: 2023947894

Translation from Macedonian into English language:
Daniela Andonovska-Trajkovska

First published in Macedonian in 2019 by Matica – Skopje
and awarded with Macedonian Literary Avant-garde in 2020
by Foundation for Cultural and Scientific Affirmation and
Presentation "Macedonia Present" Skopje, North Macedonia

CONTENTS

House of Contrasts

HOUSE OF CONTRASTS

SALTED ECHO

SHADOWS

three black shadows
were crowding into the day's gaze
like salted pebbles

they kept sitting down
on the stone
that had been bitten by the ice

from the room wide shut
from the bed with broken legs
the naked conscience emerged devastated
and lost its consciousness

SALTED PEBBLES

three black shadows
were crowding into the day's gaze
like salted pebbles

SALTED ECHO

I was walking on the edge of the rock of salt
and the empty lap under my chest
started to grow in a circle
that distances from its-own center

TEARS OF WAX

the thoughts with their heads bent down
were crawling as if they were ants
along the path spattered with black flowers
and tears of wax

- they were helping a tender voice
to climb up slowly the stairs of heavens
to the song of the cherubs

SEWED HOME

the needle of faith
was sewing someone's home
for 24 hours
just to make stitches on the smile
of a mother

her daughter's song
was hugging her tightly
around her waist
until the heavens opened

with the voice of the cherubs
the song sang itself

VOCAL CORDS OF THE SKY

A voice
Has just climbed up
The vocal cords of the sky
All alone

THE VOICE OF AN ANGEL

you are awakening the heavens
with your voice of an angel
and the pebbles are becoming aware
of the rock...

EYES FULL OF SOIL AND SOUL FULL OF SKY

The song was waking up the sky's vocal cords,
while the migraine was dancing on Earth
with thorny rose in the mouth

The sky in rupture couldn't see the Earth
and the Earth in sorrow couldn't hear the sky

And when the bird that was singing on the tree
started to give away the sky
as if it was food for the soul
the angels and the migraine
looked into each others' mournfully-blazed eyes
and finally rested in peace

With eyes full of soil
and soul full of sky
we returned home

WATER

I remain silent with the whole water in my body
with all the streams
from which the ocean cannot fall asleep
with all the braided rivers
whose roots grow upwards the course
with all the springs that cause me fever
with the sky I remain silent and
with all time
with all the blood that is running
in my words

ERYTHROCYTES IN MY EYES

I am passing by your house
with closed gaze and imprisoned song

every day on my way back home
I wipe away erythrocytes from my eyes

IMPRISONED BREATHING

with the time's rain drops
and a chamomile tea bag
I washed away the pain
that lived on the lower jaw
under that street
with unripe and loud conifers
rolling on its asphalted body

my breathing remained imprisoned
among the iron rails
of the nameless days

PATHETIC POEM

I am not who I am
when I am with you
although I am almost never with you

My poems get sick and pathetic
because you are not allowed to see
the insomnia that is crying in me
and the tears
without metaphysics
have no aesthetics

I am not who I am
when I am with you
although I am almost never with you

SALTY MOSAIC

I declare salted marks on my face
as customs duty
and I pay taxes
for the mosaic of my life

PASSPORT

I live among
a plate of lazy lasagna,
a green vase painted with flowers,
a cup of black sleepy coffee,
a board made of cork that hangs on the gaze,
a coconut pencil pot,
colored notes multiplying on the desk,
Kinder eggs toys,
desires travelling on the back seat of my car,
amethyst with a captured gaze on the Moon,
a photo with a tie and without a fracture
and the external memory
which is my passport
when I am crossing the line
to be myself

BROKEN MIRRORS

BROKEN MIRRORS

We tell the story of the human
who looks at his image
in the broken mirror of the escaped pantomime

We are what we will never be

NOTHINGNESS

A single Nothingness told me once
that the birth mark
splits our eyes from our soul

Ever since,
I always look at the navel
of the person I greet,
because I want to see whether
he is next of kin of Nothingness
that whispers to me in my womb

THE GRAPE HONEY OF OUR FINITY

We peeled out the sighs of the grape grains
We grinded the seeds of the grape honey
We squeezed until we felt pain the juices of our time

And nothing came out as we had anticipated
The juices had no water,
and the seeds had already spat out the cells
a long time ago

The wine didn't betray us,
but the line with which we used to tie the lid
over the empty room with transparent walls
did

STRETCHED SIGH

A female sigh
stretched out in the bed
to fix her upper back
which got displaced during her sleep
so she could continue living
in the second half of the dream
while she was having a hot shower
while she was combing her hair in front of the mirror
while her mind was completely blank
while she was driving from home to work
on the same road
while she remained silent in the amphitheatre
while the chairs were solving the unsolvable riddle

She kept talking incessantly
as she was explaining the theory of creation.
Nevertheless, she didn't know
whether the story had begun on her way back home
or on her way out of her home
or while she was listening to arhythmical music
when she was throwing away
the humped gazes of the day
along with the leftovers of the lunch

SIGH

A sigh
was silent in the amphitheatre
while the little chairs were solving
an unsolvable puzzle

A sigh
was talking incessantly
after the lunch
when she was throwing away
the humped gazes of the day
along with the leftovers of the lunch

VERTICAL LOVE

there is a vertical line
that never changes its position
you can punch her stomach as much as you like
you can pull her hair
or stick your tongue out
you can dance in front of her
by standing on your arms
scream at her to make sure she hears you
let your blood flow in front of her
change your name
breathe in her neck
kiss her shadow
tickle her to make her smile
you can look into her eyes as much as you like
so that she can recognize you
you can do to her whatever you like
and to your heart's content
to make her bend towards you
but she will still be the wall
between you and the world

VERTICAL MIRROR

there is a vertical line
that never changes its position
you can press her vein as much as you like
just to make her blood flow
you can look into her eyes as much as you like
to make her hear your name
you can do to her whatever you like
and how much as you like
to domesticate her
nevertheless she will continue to be the mirror
that draws the finest wrinkles on your face

STONE

There is a stone I circumvent every day
but it keeps returning in my palm
to keep me awake
in the process of my birth

DOMESTICATED WORDS

THE ART OF LIVING

With my eyes wide shut,
I was listening to the legato of your thoughts
slowly sliding over
the white and black piano keys of life

I was watching you
dressing the words into new skin
and I witnessed how the paramecium of meaning
started turning into multicellular organism which
breathed with its own lungs

I was dreaming about the metaphors
from which the lightnings
were learning the art of the souls' whisper
and I kept waking up

In the circled colors of pointillism I shut you
to show me how with fast
and sharp movements
you write about moments
no one could ever have

and when I wanted to tell you
that you reminded me of something
that I had within me a long time ago
your words got stuck into the bird's throat

Do not let us be nude, I cried,
do not let us be alone with no art of living

DOMESTICATED WORDS

Inspired by "The Little Prince" by Antoine de Saint-Exupéry

I was giving you the essential oils of the words
every morning
to keep you hydrated
but you wanted me to have you
in the bell jar of my glimpse
because you were afraid
of other people's breathing

And then I thought
that you will kill all of my volcanoes
with which I am breathing into the century's womb
as if they are my lungs
and I left you
so you could feel the pain
of the heated chlorophyll

I see your sky differently now
when I am finding myself out of myself
with a serpent under my tongue
a landscape with watery roses in my eyes
and a thorny flower on my lips

I am yours, my darling,
and I am finally coming home
with grey hair and wrinkled heart.

CELLULAR BREATHING OF THE SILENCE

I was holding your arteries in my hands
and I felt the oxygen of pain
running through my body
while you were breaking my hips
with your legs wide open
because you didn't want me to have your image
in the mirror

I was awakened by Edit Piaf's square
that observed Gala who was playing
with the colors of life one night
wanting to kill the dullness in the straight line
She invented the pure art
while the Eluard's handwriting
watched the time that was melting
in Dali's Persistence of Memory
looking for the recipe of eternity

And you pressed my eyes again
damn you, with the darkness' open palms
to prevent me anticipate
whether I will touch my pointed mustaches
drawn by the eyes that penetrate in me
when I wake up late in the afternoon,
or I will touch the plasticide horns,
the crown with dirt under the nails
or the beggar's stick of the carbonated words
that want to get out of my veins
and meet themselves

CRUMBLED WORDS

I shook off the breadcrumps from the table sheet
and I missed the moment of shaking off my words, too
...
And when I felt my thought
stuck in my throat later on
in labour pains and shut sky
I saw sparrows with full bellies
and beaks hung on the dream
having a nap on the line
on which the sky and the Earth
are touching each other
in an infinite number of dots

NUDE SILENCE

I dress up the paper
with your naked body

TRANSPARENT SYNAPSES

I bit the apple only once
and I got pinched by the word
from the pentagram inside
and from the tree up above your head
I told you that you are nude
and you don't need anybody
and you can give birth to Adam all by yourself
and I gave you leaves
so you could imprison yourself in a cage
in a walnut shell – with transparent synapses

A POEM FOR THE SILENCE

As we breathe with the little flame
that crawls on the wall
so it can learn about the stone
and while the word is inventing the meaning,
unknown signs are starting to expand our irises
and they slowly flow back into the river.

As we write on the wall
with the alphabet of the soul
the composer of life
hunts the finest musical notes
and gives birth to the poem of the silence

MUSIC

The light sees us with our-own eyes
with an open sky and hands reaching for God

without keys and lines
the notes are singing inside of us
lifting the chest of the man
that exhales us

the universe creates perfect music in us
when we feel that we are not alone

TORN LETTERS

One "I" cannot look into its own "Eye"
because the image in the mirror
is the folded side of the paper
that sees us
with the microseconds of illiterate time

the time that cannot write
the time that cannot count

HUMAN DROPS

I love to sit by the window
with all of my eternity
and to watch the multiple faces of God
that are running down
on the human's soul of glass

I love to see the sky crying happily
as it fertilizes the cracked valley
with soil in its gaze

But what I love most is to sit
on the inner side of my vigilance
because all human drops
live there in the amniotic fluid of the century
and that is the only place in which my "I"
breathes with its lungs

WINGS IN A FOAM BUBBLE

SILENT VERSES

The look at the window
is a memory of the sea
which spills out
of the morning cup of tea

THE WORD'S SILHOUETTE

The silhouette of the word
that looks for its own image
in the mirror of the night
leans on the eyelids of the window
and inhabits the look over a cup of tea
in a teary timeless morning

WORDLESS POEM

The two elbows on the window's frame
that is sitting on the stone of the word
are metonymy of a gaze
thrust at the bottom of a poem
which has a face
but has no words

DROWNED SILENCE

The words were running down
on the teary windows.

They were saying hello to each other,
they were throwing white gloves at each other,
they were punching each other
with their clenched fists,
they were aiming and shooting at each other,
they were falling down and
they were instantly getting on their feet, and then
they were hugging and kissing each other and
they were saying good bye for good,... and then
they were hugging and kissing again,
and getting on their feet,
and falling down,
and shooting,
and aiming,
and punching,
and challenging, and then
they were saying hello to each other again - in a loop

I closed the windows from the past
the pink sugar wool stick on which my memories were
melting
from the touch of my thoughts
has just opened a hole under my tongue.
The glass drowned
along with the wool and the ice.

ALPHABET

My alphabet was born on the knife
that cuts the umbilical cord

POEM

in the blue look of the ocean
in the deep breathing of the mountain
in the vocal cords of the fish
in the pearl's dream
a poem was born

LOVED POEM

the seconds of the future in the past without present
squeeze into the keyhole of a home
with no address

there lives a poem
in which I keep falling in love with
over and over again
although I know her

I found myself all alone in her gaze
but another woman has got her initials

and that she is mine
as much as everybody else's
hurts like hell

...
Fall asleep, my dear poem,
all over my transparent body
and don't think that I am far away from you
The truth is that I am with you even when I am not
and when I don't want to love you
then I love you the most
and it is then that I can't tell
where I stop and where you start,
because we are one

Fall asleep, my poem, so that we can be alone
Me - without a body
you - without initials

NO ADDRESS

between a grain of sand and a body of desire
a watery sigh which is stuck in the fairy tales
is rolling

there is nothing
except for love and poetry

WINGS IN A FOAM BUBBLE

you keep telling me to squeeze to become me
to squeeze the dream to be able to see the reality
to squeeze the time and to live in the seconds
to squeeze the verses so I could write music
to squeeze the words and to give my thought space
to squeeze the universe
for the Milky Way to burst in an explosion
you keep telling me to squeeze if I want to become me

but I am a bad disciple
and I know that I can't squeeze the word
to extract the essential oils of the thought,
nor I can squeeze the moment
from which the whole time of humanity will leak out.
And I wonder
will I ever learn to squeeze myself,
so I could spread my wings in a bubble foam?

A POEM FOR THE POEM

A poem should have a perfect seed-like body
even when she has got freckles from the sun
and when she borrows the hedgehog's attire
and when she pulls the stomach in
in front of the trigger
and when she makes smokey balloons
with her tongue
and when she holds a thermometer in her mouth
and when she drinks up the acidified apple
and when she wakes up between the sleepy seeds
and when she gets drunk by the soulmates' love
and when she drinks the morning coffee
with shaggy hair
A poem should be beautiful even when she is ugly
A poem should have a soul

UNIFORMED TOYS

MOVING IMAGES

We get itchy by the amniotic sac
folded down with 2 grams of naphthalene
and cast under the rug

we feel upon us the weight of the chandelier
which pledges fidelity
in the house in which everyone hides
in their own room

We get blind by the television
that like a vacuum cleaner
collects all of our images
that we had ripped from ourselves

The images left their home in quest for themselves
and we were left in the house
with our stoned gaze on their cracked heels

THE CHAIN OF ETERNITY

In my DNA I see your tail crawling
looking for a hole
to get outside

THE CHAIN OF THE 21 CENTURY

When the black Labrador
lifted his right leg tangled
in the long chain of the night
a scratchy scream started to leak
from the throat of the eyeless wall.

The chain felt the same
as when he was killing the toy of the little Syrian boy
as when he crumbled the eye apples
of the classroom in Peshawar
as when he was taking by force
the doll of the girl from India
as he was counting to 22 in Yemen
as he was advertising the nudity of the soul
on the social media of alienation
for the purpose of earning 1 cent
with each left click of the mouse
on the lost seconds in the whirl of the addiction
as when he was hiding the life
from the cancerous face of the day,
just to make a profit from the halls without empathy.

The word cried after him
and the chain unclasped his palms
because he knew that the neighbours
look at him with double eyes.

The Labrador
was still barking in front of the door
because that was the only place
where the metal name tag
that hung on the red dog collar around its neck
was flashing astonishingly.

YELLOW INSOMNIA

When I go to bed late in the night
in the town with 80000 citizens
and 5 main streets
the stretched tendon reminds me
of the yesterday's marathon
financed by the big tadpoles
And I cannot fall a sleep

When I go to bed late in the night
the popped jugular on my neck
reminds me
of the cat-and-mouse game
that is going in circles
around my yellow insomnia

When I go to bed late in the night
my thought with strident handwriting
starts to write me messages
on yellow sticky lineless notes
just to tell me that she cannot fall asleep.

UNIFORMED TOYS

The night
in which all of the t-shirts must wear the same logo
will eat us all
before the red alarm takes us all

That is the reason
why the toys have nobody to play with

RED, YELLOW, GREEN

I have a sore neck and shoulder blade pain
from the watchful yellow insomnia that sees
the world in its red alarm zone

The green sky
will never let us go
to flow
into our own "I"
that no longer recognizes
the colours of the traffic light

MECHANICAL GRINS

A thought was hanging
on the sharp edge of the insomnia
with only one hand.
The Great Canyon was waiting for her
with mouth wide open
and the bald eagle
was measuring the hollow
with its wings wide spread

The rangers with the horseshoes of death
were going down the canyon like ants
and the double-eyed tourists
wanted to frame the moment
in the forgetful machine

Noone ever saw the thought
hung on the sharp edge of the insomnia
nor the fact that she was feeding
the comedian with his winded up grin
and teary clock wheels
in the time of mechanical grins

AWAKENED THOUGHT

No one ever noticed the thought
that won't live long enough to see
another ark of repentance

AMAZED THOUGHT

My amazed thought
suddenly stopped as she was crossing the zebra
and all of a sudden,
all the cars in which the invertebrates' egos
were travelling by
stopped the moment they saw me
all the pedestrians that didn't know
where they were going,
all the street dogs with misty vocal cords,
all the counters that pay off in installments
the workers' sweat
and the homeless man who has just woken
from the humped dream of the toothless day
stopped as well...

My amazed thought
suddenly stopped
as she was crossing the zebra
and all my "I" that couldn't say
where they were coming from
nor where they were going to,
stopped, as well,
on the pedestrian lines
that were curved enough
so anybody could stay on them
in an upright position
in spite of the gravity
of their own thoughts...

MOM, WHO AM I?

Mom, who am I? –
asked me the three-year-old little voice
as we were crossing the street hand in hand
on the pedestrian cross.
My thought was startled
and suddenly stopped on the zebra crossing.

I stop very often at the same place even today
in the middle of the carriageway of the forgotten "I"-s
Even today, the very same little voice pulls me down
to make me bend towards him to hear his whisper:
Mom, who am I?

CainEthics

The two ventricles close the door for the two atriums
and the blood runs out of the pores

The towers without windows look at us,
but we are crying on the inner side of the wall.

The mole visits its newborn children
and digs their eyes out.

The river being jealous of the sky
muddies its waters

The watery towels that hang on our shoulder blades
are filled with the blood of the fallen Abel.

Our heels hurt us so much
that we curse our own steps...

HOUSE OF CONTRASTS

ROLLED GAME

The game that you and I play
drinks the springs of the fire
which spreads between two hills
and rolls on the three dots of the sentence
in the labour pain of the universe

YIN AND YANG

Your words are as soft as the first snow
You keep the children's laugh gently in your palm
without causing a single snowflake to melt

               My words are heavy and sharp like knives
               when they walk they sink into their own steps

Your breathing is as deep as the wind's
you lift the sea up as a child
when you want to play with it

               My breathing is as shallow
               as my awakening
               I am short of breath when I have to blow away the reel
               of creating

Your breathing is as long
as the legato in the piano player's thought
you fill with red blood cells
the thin skin of the words

               My breathing is as shallow
               as the staccato of the dotted insomnia
               I fill with white blood cells
               the long sentence of the looks

Your thoughts are talkative
they argue aloud
about the philosophy of breathing

               My words are angled
               they write themselves down
               on the five-line music notebook of nonspeaking

You are laughing while retelling the story
about the white night of your summer

               I am crying while looking at the black story
               of my winter.

THE WORLDS OF LIGHT

In my binary world
the light fights with its own absence
to defeat itself

> In your magical world
> the light breaks down in colors
> and lives in its own presence

My metonymical and your metaphorical world
are living together
in a book with a laser print
This gives the sun freckles too
When it looks directly into its eyes

THE DOLL WITH WINDED UP STEPS

the sleepy footprints in the hall that flashes
and the upholstered walls full of CO_2
are my witnesses
that I didn't want to be your toy
that cries upon touch
I didn't want you to sew me strings on my palms
I didn't want you to talk to me from my stomach
nor to wind up steps on my back

But I didn't say anything
when I put down my head
next to your thoughts

CALCIFICATE OF TIME

The night of the X-rays
reminded me of the broken promises
that healed in malunion,
of my persistent attempts to convince you that
you are the spinal cord of our home,
and your arrogant denial of the marrow of our
conversation,
of my not-so-distant complaints about my sore shoulder,
and your claim that the discus hernia provoked by other
people's looks on me is killing you,
of the fact that even if you don't take your calcium pill
before going to bed
the cartilage of our youth
will remain imprisoned
in the symmetrical calcification of time

BROKEN IMAGES

My house had fractures on two spots
and they were both laying down on the lower jaw
and they both kept silent between two iron rails
and they both couldn't sleep at night

                                        but not because of the pain

and I was locking, oh God, I was locking the door
whenever I would go out
and I threw the key in the ditch by the road
                                  but I kept going home
                     and I kept putting the iron into my mouth
                      and I squeezed words through my teeth
                       I clenched a fist with broken phalanx

I put my thoughts in a blender every night
and went down the stairs inaudibly
so I wouldn't wake myself up
each night, oh, God, I grinded salty grains from my
cheeks
and each night, I gave birth to Her
and I was waking up in my house again
between the two sleepless nights it was Her that I had
between the two broken images – out of my own image I
ran

HOUSE OF CONTRASTS

When I open the front door to enter my home
                    through the back door my shadow goes out
and no one sees the flood in my working room because of the
blossomed orchids on my living room's window
                    and no one can ever feel the scent of pine trees
            that is coming from my back window

and no one, no one at all
can see the invisible resin of the past
                        laid on the coffee table where I serve
            Greek coffee, Turkish delight and German chocolate
and when I speak aloud in my sleeplessness
                        no one, no one at all can hear
                        how the day crumbles in me
and puts the pieces again all at once like X-rays do
that no one
will ever point a finger at my naked body

MODERN TIME

the silence lays down on the walls
and breathes with the dreamt time's notes

in the room with walls made of glass
in the imprisoned hope hidden under the table
our modern time lives

ABSENT TIME

in the room without doors and windows
a lonely time lives

it pulls the blanket up to its nose in the darkness
so it could watch the advertisements
for the "all inclusive" poverty,
the broken capillaries of bulimia
and the bank accounts of anorexia

in the room without doors and windows
our absent time lives

AUTISTIC TIME

it doesn't respond when you are addressing it
nor when you call its name
nor when you want to ask it something

but it knows your name
and your home address
and your birth date
and the number of your ID
and it can calculate the day of your death

and when you think that there is no one in the room
you will recognize it
by the swaying curtain behind you
in the room for which you have no key
our autistic time lives

NO ONE LIVES WHERE THE GLASS IS IMMECULATELY CLEAN

the torn sighs in which the essential oils
of the eternity are being held
are running down the chilled window

no one lives
in the place
where the glass is immaculately clean

THE BEDROOM ALWAYS TELLS YOU
THE TRUTH

the bedroom always tells you the truth
if you look attentively at the wrinkles of the bed sheet

He has turned his back on Her
while She embraces what does not exist in Him

He turns towards Her in a fetal position
She takes Him into Her womb without giving it a second
thought
although She is half His size

She turns Her back on Him wanting to get inside His
circle

He caresses His Ego
and takes what belongs to Him completely:
the empty side of the bed

the bedroom always tells you the truth
all you have to do
is to look for the wrinkles
on the inner side of your sleep

THE HOUSE THAT SHINES

In the middle of the half-closed gazes
and the square in the city center
In the middle of the coffee sips and the chess game
under the time without watches
In the middle of the shop windows
full of pictures of the past
and the moving stairs that go nowhere

                                            a hidden house lives

Moss of sighs grows on her skin
while two sweaty bodies are burning in the heart
of the hidden house that lives under my skin

HOUSE OF CARDS

The fire that drips its flames
down the roof of the house made of cards
fills all the volcanoes of a man's planet

There are neither wild nor domestic animals,
nor baobabs, roses, foxes, nor snakes
- only – He himself, the Earth and the sky

There is a homeless young woman
living under his skin
Therefore his skin is always young,
and his volcanoes create life on Earth
with lava of words

TWO KEYS

I live with a cat
that multiplies in my dream
and takes all shapes of time
in the ruins between Parthenon and Heraclea
and the Templars and Michelangelo
and the Grate Depression
and the rebels of our collective memory

and when I see all of our lives
in the green eyes of the darkness
that purrs quietly on the porch of the house
the keyhole starts to release
and frees all of the passwords
that we have been locking ourselves in

and you tell me:
"Look how the time is being unlocked
with two wooden keys only:
the first one is me,
and the second one is you".

and then I release that shadow
that meows in the dream
and let her wander all around the city
so she can find the keys
hidden in the five-line music notebook
the one that is me,
and the other one that is you

THE LITTLE PAPER HUMANS AND GOD

There are no homes in this city...
only houses from which humans made of paper
go out every day
they sit down in the little newspaper boats
to go as far as they can go
to be further from the others
to be closer to themselves

Every night, the humans made of paper
are coming back to the keyhole
cursing the day
that does not last long enough
so that they could find themselves.

Every day, their profanities thrown
among words of lead
that are falling apart
from the newspapers of the past
flow in the river
looking for God

WINTER MOSAIC

The cells of a winter,
For which I know for fact how many crystals
has drawn on the eyelashes of the waiting,
and with how many melted snowflakes
has kissed me while I sleep,
have been gathering together in my equinox

They are going down my vertical "I"
so they can see themselves
on the other side of the mirror
- with all the question marks that are waking up
on the foggy surface of breathing

They are being placed like pebbles
in the mosaic of what has already happened
And there – the darkness inhabits the irises
because she knows
that the dotted image of the memory
will never be complete
without the shadow's gaze on it.

FAKE MUSIC NOTES

The fake smiles
are rolling down the podium
of our overeaten time
that sticks 20 Euros on the forehead
of the lame clarinetist
and he knows very well
that stilted suits cannot dance
in tune with the 7/8 meter
only the ones with a soul can do that
- therefore he sells them fake music notes
on a shiny paper

EVERY DAY ON SHIROK SOKAK

Every day on Shirok Sokak[1]
curious looks are having a walk in the same way

The salesmen are washing out the days that have passed
by
and let them run on the black tiles
that no one dares to step on
because the Orthopedic Ward announced
they had no beds available

There are Pinches, Labradors, Samoyeds,
Shih Tzu, Husks, Maltesers
running around, wanting to be seen
and the owners with golden chains on their neck are
barking after them

Pupils in a rush with a backpack full of theory.
Slowed down students forgotten in theory.
Branded professors with exclamation marks next to their
titles.
Graduated saleswomen
with no facial expressions.

Separated quasi-politicians:
the ones that are sitting in the smoking area,
and the others – in the part for nonsmokers.
And they are the same, but their coffee is separated by a
plexiglass

Lonely faces are sitting on the wooden circle
in front of the Center of Culture
and they see their youth
passing by them

Suited old men
support their-own age
on rusted bikes with the YU mark on them

---

1 The most famous promenade street in Bitola, North Macedonia

Young mothers are pushing their nonexistent graduation
diplomas
in baby carts

Men are looking for a job
in a sip of black coffee from 12.00 pm. to 3.00pm.

                              Mobile phones are staring at themselves
                              while they are in the company of others

Children dressed up as adults
pull strings off their parents' coats.

                    A begging palm and a baby – at Magnolia Square
              three small ones, laughing and playful – in front of Vero
                         a humped one – at the Stone Bridge

Every day on Shirok Sokak is the same
On Shirok Sokak – nothing new

BIOGRAPHY

Daniela Andonovska-Trajkovska (1979, Bitola, Republic of North Macedonia) is a poetess, author, scientist, editor in chief of two literary magazines in North Macedonia, literary critic, doctor of pedagogy, university professor at the University "Kliment Ohridski" Bitola (Faculty of Education), a member of the Macedonian Writers' Association; Macedonian Science Society – Bitola; Slavic Academy for Literature and Art in Varna – Bulgaria, and Bitola Literary Circle. She was president of the Macedonian Science Society Editorial Council and now – a head of the Linguistics and Literature Department at the Macedonian Science Society – Bitola. She has published two books of stories, 9 poetry books, one book for children, a book of literary criticism in Macedonian and 3 academic and scientific books that are part of the curriculum at the university where she works, and over 100 scientific articles. She has also 6 poetry books published in English, Italian, Arabic and Romanian language in India, United Arab Emirates, Italy, and Romania. She has also published her translations from English into Macedonian and vice versa in North Macedonia, Italy and Netherland (7 poetry books and many articles). She has won several important awards for literature: "Krste Chachanski (2018); "Karamanov" for "Electronic Blood" (2019); Macedonian Literary Avant-garde for "House of Contrasts" (2020); "Abduvali Qutbiddin" (2020, Uzbekistan); Premio Mondiale "Tulliola-Renato Filippelli" in Italy for "Electronic Blood" (2021); Award of excellence "City of Galateo - Antonio De Ferrariis" (Italy); Award for Literary Criticism in 2022, Poetry Award "Dritero Agioli" (Albania, 2023); Naji Naaman Award in 2023; Poetry Award "Mihai Eminescu", a Golden Medal and a recognition as ambassador of culture in Romania by the Mihai Eminescu Academy (2023) and "Aco Shopov" for poetry (the most important national poetry prize by Macedonian Writers' Association in 2021). Her poetry has been translated and published into more than 40 world languages.

Books by Daniela Andonovska-Trajkovska

Poetry

A Word about the Word
Poem about the Margins
Black Dot
Footprints
Three
House of Contrasts
Electronic Blood in Macedonian (Radovish: Center for Culture),
     "Aco Karamanov"
Electronic Blood in Arabic (United Arab Emirates}
Electronic Blood in English (India)
Math Poetry
Dandelion Cadence in English (India)
Walking on an Aerial Line
Soul full of Sky in Italian and English (Italy)
Omuletiii de Hartie si Dumnezeu (Little Paper Men and God), translated into
     Romanian by Constantin Severin

Prose

Coffee, Tea and a Red Sky
Deconstruction of the Void

Translations

Mai Van Phan and Raed Anis Al-Jishi (2020), *New Year Bath*, (Editor Borche Panov), translation into Macedonian by Daniela Andonovska-Trajkovska, Center for Culture, "Aco Karamanov" Radovish

The Fifth Season: Anthology of the Karamanov Poetry Meetings (2020), translation into Macedonian by Daniela Andonovska-Trajkovska, Center for Culture, "Aco Karamanov" Radovish

Borce Panov, *Underground Apple*, translation into Macedonian by Daniela Andonovska-Trajkovska, Published in English in 2021 by Demer Press, Netherland, and in English and Macedonian in 2022 by Matica, North Macedonia

Daniela Andonovska-Trajkovska (2021), *Electronic Blood*, (published by Cyberwit)

Claudia Piccinno (2021), *A Hole of Light into the Cathedral* (Editor and co-translator Borche Panov), translation into Macedonian by Daniela Andonovska-Trajkovska, Center for Culture, "Aco Karamanov" Radovish

Borche Panov: *Sculpture of Breathing*, translation into Macedonian by Daniela Andonovska-Trajkovska and Claudia Picinno, 2022

Constantin Severin, *The Lives of the Painters* (2022), translation into Macedonian by Daniela Andonovska-Trajkovska, Center for Culture, "Aco Karamanov" Radovish

Jose Eduardo Degrazia (2022), *Condemned Cities*, translation into Macedonian by: Daniela Andonovska-Trajkovska, Center for Culture, "Aco Karamanov" Radovish

Literary Criticism

Literary Criticism (Bitola: Bitola's Literary Cycle, 2022)

www.ingramcontent.com/pod-product-compliance
Lightning Source LLC
Chambersburg PA
CBHW021344090426
42742CB00008B/745